Accompaniment CD

SOLOS
for the
VIOLA
PLAYER

With Piano Accompaniment

Selected and Edited by
PAUL DOKTOR

On the accompaniment recording:
STEFANIE JACOB and LAURA WARD
pianists

ED 2307-C

ISBN 978-1-61780-610-0

G. SCHIRMER, Inc.

DISTRIBUTED BY

HAL•LEONARD®
CORPORATION
7777 W. BLUEMOUND RD. P.O. BOX 13819 MILWAUKEE, WI 53213

www.schirmer.com
www.halleonard.com

CONTENTS

Pianists on the CD:
[1] Stefanie Jacob
[2] Laura Ward

PREFACE

The purpose of this anthology is to make available to the viola player a substantial body of work which can best help him to bring forth the peculiarly expressive nature of the viola as a solo instrument, and the special eloquence of the modern style of viola playing. A definitely new conception of this instrument's place in the world of musical art in general, and of string performance in particular, is making its way among musicians and audiences alike. The special genius of the viola is expressed in the word *cantilena* or *bel canto*, a style for which its sonorities are magnificently suited. With this in mind I have chosen the music for this anthology from the great arched phrases of Bach to the American folk song Shenandoah. The aim is the same: to produce the singing style, the plastic phrase, the dynamic of song-speech. This, of course, doesn't mean that compositions of faster tempi have been ignored. On the contrary, the player will find some lovely works which disprove some old-fashioned judgments that the viola is merely an instrument to portray melancholy, mourning, tears, and sighs. The viola player who cannot put sunshine into his playing is not giving full scope to his instrument.

The present edition is aimed to be of assistance to:
STUDENTS, by introducing them to more valuable and enticing literature;
AMATEURS, by bringing to them solo pieces they may have known, but which until now they had no way of playing on the viola;
ARTIST/PERFORMERS, by giving them hitherto unpublished shorter works, either suitable as encores or for the program itself.

Quite naturally, such a collection must also contain transcriptions. I did refrain from using compositions overly well known as "belonging" to another instrument, be it even one as closely related as the violin. But pieces, such as those by Marais and Caix d'Hervelois which were originally written for viola da gamba or the tenor viol (the forerunner of the viola), cannot even be regarded as transcriptions. The Brahms and Wolf songs, as well as the spirituals and folksongs, or, for that matter, the Romance by Méhul, are included because the viola is perhaps the instrument closest related to the human voice. From my own teaching experience I felt the need of such pieces to make the viola player aware that it is the real voice-like singing tone that we should attain. Bearing this in mind the player will find his technique merging happily with the qualities of his instrument. The result can only be expressiveness and pleasure, and the aim of this collection will have been fulfilled.

The editor's thanks are extended to Milton Halpern without whose helpful initiative this anthology might not have been written; to Dr. Egon Kornauth for his thoughtful cooperation in preparing the piano part for numbers 1, 3, 4, 7, 13, 14 and 15; and to Sydney Beck for the permission of using part of his edition of Beethoven's Notturno, which is published in its entirety by G. Schirmer, Inc.

PAUL DOKTOR

ABOUT THE ENHANCED CD

In addition to piano accompaniments playable on both your CD player and computer, this enhanced CD also includes tempo adjustment software for computer use only. This software, known as Amazing Slow Downer, was originally created for use in pop music to allow singers and players the freedom to independently adjust both tempo and pitch elements. Because we believe there may be valuable educational use for these features in classical and theatre music, we have included this software as a tool for both the teacher and student. For quick and easy installation instructions of this software, please see below.

In recording a piano accompaniment we necessarily must choose one tempo. Our choice of tempo, phrasing, ritardandos, and dynamics is carefully considered. But by the nature of recording, it is only one option.

However, we encourage you to explore your own interpretive ideas, which may differ from our recordings. This new software feature allows you to adjust the tempo up and down without affecting the pitch. We recommend that this new tempo adjustment feature be used with care and insight. Ideally, you will be using these recorded accompaniments and Amazing Slow Downer for practice only.

The audio quality may be somewhat compromised when played through the Amazing Slow Downer. This compromise in quality will not be a factor in playing the CD audio track on a normal CD player or through another audio computer program.

INSTALLATION FROM DOWNLOAD:

For Windows (XP, Vista or 7):
1. Download and save the .zip file to your hard drive.
2. Extract the .zip file.
3. Open the "ASD Lite" folder.
4. Double-click "setup.exe" to run the installer and follow the on-screen instructions.

For Macintosh (OSX 10.4 and up):
1. Download and save the .dmg file to your hard drive.
2. Double-click the .dmg file to mount the "ASD Lite" volume.
3. Double-click the "ASD Lite" volume to see its contents.
4. Drag the "ASD Lite" application into the Application folder.

INSTALLATION FROM CD:

For Windows (XP, Vista or 7):
1. Load the CD-ROM into your CD-ROM drive.
2. Open your CD-ROM drive. You should see a folder named "Amazing Slow Downer." If you only see a list of tracks, you are looking at the audio portion of the disk and most likely do not have a multi-session capable CD-ROM.
3. Open the "Amazing Slow Downer" folder.
4. Double-click "setup.exe" to install the software from the CD-ROM to your hard disk. Follow the on-screen instructions to complete installation.
5. Go to "Start," "Programs" and find the "Amazing Slow Downer Lite" application. Note: To guarantee access to the CD-ROM drive, the user should be logged in as the "Administrator."

For Macintosh (OSX 10.4 or higher):
1. Load the CD-ROM into your CD-ROM drive.
2. Double-click on the data portion of the CD-ROM (which will have the Hal Leonard icon in red and be named as the book).
3. Open the "Amazing OS X" folder.
4. Double-click the "ASD Lite" application icon to run the software from the CD-ROM, or copy this file to your hard drive and run it from there.

MINIMUM SOFTWARE REQUIREMENTS:

For Windows (XP, Vista or 7):
Pentium Processor; Windows XP, Vista, or 7; 8 MB Application RAM; 8x Multi-Session CD-ROM drive

For Macintosh (OS X 10.4 or higher):
Power Macintosh or Intel Processor; Mac OS X 10.4 or higher; MB Application RAM; 8x Multi-Session CD-ROM drive